His Grace

His Grace

GLENDA STONEBACK

Copyright © 2003 by Glenda Stoneback.

ISBN: Softcover   1-4134-2610-7

All rights reserved. No part of this book may be reproduced or transmitted in any form or by any means, electronic or mechanical, including photocopying, recording, or by any information storage and retrieval system, without permission in writing from the copyright owner.

This book was printed in the United States of America.

To order additional copies of this book, contact:
Xlibris Corporation
1-888-795-4274
www.Xlibris.com
Orders@Xlibris.com

Contents

ACKNOWLEDGEMENTS 13

Part One

CHRIST WITHIN ME 17
THE LOVE LETTER 19
ELECTION DAY 21
SALVATION 23
DELIVERANCE 24
MIRACLES 25
BE STILL 27
THE ONCE AND FOREVER KING 29
REFUGE 31
CONVICTED 32
THE MESSENGER 33
DONNA'S DOLPHINS 35
FAITH OF A CHILD 37
WARFARE 39
MARTHA AND MARY 40
LIGHTHOUSE 41
SERVANTS OF THE LORD 42
PROVERBS 31 43
NO TIME FOR PROVERBS 31 45
REVIVAL 47
REJECTED 49

LIFE SAVIOR 51
YOU WERE THERE 53
PREPARE THE WAY 55
HE HAS NOT FORGOTTEN 57
WORLDS APART 59
BLUEPRINT 61
DRAW NEAR 62
OASIS 63
ONE WORD 65
RICH LITTLE POOR GIRL 67
THROUGH THE FIRE 69
WHAT A FRIEND 70
PONDERING 72
LONELY 73

Part Two

.... 76
MY FAMILY BESIDE ME 77
OUR FAMILY QUILT 78
CHILDREN 80
LITTLE FEET 81
FIRSTBORN 82
LITTLE MISSIONARY 84
THE HANDS OF TIME 86
HOMECOMING 87
LITTLE ONE 88
SURRENDER 89
MOM 90
DADDY 91
SISTERS IN CHRIST 92

A WORLD OF INFLUENCE 93
RESUME 94
LIFE HAPPENS HERE 96
THE DANCE 98

Part Three

THE WORLD AROUND ME 101
WILL I HAVE TO STAND? 102
TRUTH IS TRUTH 104
A PERFECT WORLD 106
MADELINE'S LEGACY 107
HEAVEN'S CHILD 108
SEPTEMBER 11, 2001 109
WHO IS THIS GOD? 110
EVERYBODY BOWS 112
LINE IT UP 113
THE FOURTH OF JULY 114
A CLOSER LOOK 115
TO SPEAK 116
DEBATE 117
LONGING 118

Dedication

This book is dedicated with love to
my husband Philip and our four precious gifts,
Brett, Jodie, Sean and Simon.

*"Because Your lovingkindness is
better than life, my lips will praise You."*
Psalm 63:3

Acknowledgements

Thank You, Lord for every blessing and trial,
because I know that You work all things together
for good for those who love You and are called
according to Your purpose. (Romans 8:28)

Mom, for loving everything I write, even when I don't, and for not letting me give up.

Darla Mulhall, for sharing Christ with me on that Tuesday night in '97. You know I am eternally grateful!

Pastor Randy Gaumer, for the boldness in your messages that challenges, convicts, instructs and encourages me so I can grow in my faith.

Robyn Henning, for your wise counsel and solid teaching.

Theda Steil, for being an awesome Titus 2 woman, an example to me of true humility and service, and a true friend who does not turn away when she doesn't know the answers, but offers prayer and encouragement.

Erich Lukas, for sharing the truth, exposing the lies and sending out my poetry in his newsletter.

And my family, just for being you. I love you.

Part One

Christ Within Me

My Testimony

"Why was it such a happy ending if they died?"

This was my question after attending the drama, "Bridge of Blood" at First Baptist Church in Perkasie, Pa. The pastor's wife told me the people who killed the missionaries had later come to know the Lord.

But the missionaries died! I reminded her. She gave me an answer to ponder. "The missionaries went to heaven." She said it without a doubt. It must be nice to know that, I thought.

A few days later, my new friend Darla explained that I could not get to heaven on my own, and that is why Jesus Christ was crucified. He took the punishment for all my sin. All I had to do was accept His gift and trust in Him for my salvation. I asked Jesus into my heart that very night.

The best part is, His offer is available to everyone who believes in Him. We have that guarantee in writing!

"For God so loved the world, that He gave
His only begotten Son, that whoever **believes**
in Him shall not perish, but have eternal life." John 3:16

"We love because He first loved us." 1 John 4:19

The Love Letter

She was a lonely girl, betrayed
By all she knew and was afraid
To give her heart away.
She looked upon her shelf and found
A book that she had kept around,
Though only for display.

She opened it one day to seek
The answers to her life so bleak
And found herself engaged.
The book not only held advice
But a map to Paradise
Unveiling page by page.

Through generations' lives she read,
By poetry her heart was fed,
By prophecy, amazed.
But when she reached the book of John,
As her eyes continued on,
Her heart was set ablaze.

Tears fell as she began to see
The awful pain and agony
Love prompted Him to bear.
He hung upon the guilty tree,
Though wholly innocent was He,
His love had held Him there.

No longer would she feel so lost,
For One had paid the precious cost
And freed her from her sin.
Her heart rejoiced today instead,
For, just as His love letter said,
She now belonged to Him.

"Choose this day whom you will serve." Joshua 24:15

Election Day

My story

In the dim-lit stairwell
Two women sat alone.
One a firm believer,
One who's never known.

The loving voice was sharing,
The story did unfold
Revealing to a lost child
A gift more pure than gold.

With wonder she received
The news of Jesus' love
And promise of eternity
With Him in heaven above.

Her head bowed down, her heart aflame,
She received His gift of grace,
Her guilt and fear dissolving,
With peace and joy replaced.

In the dim-lit stairwell
Two sisters sat in tears,
Both of them believing,
Since one had shown no fear.

"But all things become visible when they are exposed by the light." Ephesians 5:13

Salvation

How blessed the transition
From the darkness of the night.
My weary eyes straining,
Adjusting to the light.

From fog of doubt He brought me
To hope of future bliss
The present peace and joy
Of perfect love's forgiveness.

My hazy lack of understanding
Turned to clarity of heart,
A blur brought into focus,
His grace a work of art.

In gratitude and love I live
To serve Him evermore;
To follow where He leads me,
My life in Him secure.

"For the gate is small and the way is narrow that leads to life and there are few who find it." Matthew 7:14

Deliverance

He longed to break these chains of mine
But I would not obey.
I though so foolishly that I
alone could find my way.

Repeatedly my ways have failed
To free me from this curse,
But holding back the glory due
To him was even worse.

But now He's straightened out my path,
Though narrow it may be.
By trusting in His master plan,
I know at last I'm free!

*"In the world you will have tribulation, but take courage,
I have overcome the world." John 16:33*

Miracles

I believe in miracles,
I know I always will.
For even in this darkened world,
The Lord is present still.

People often question me
On how I can believe
When senseless acts of violence
Are causing us to grieve.

No one seems to care at all
For sanctity of life
And families are torn apart
By selfishness and strife.

Christ Himself has witnessed
All the trials we face today.
And, walking on this earth by choice,
He knew the price He'd pay.

He offered up His ransom,
That which I could not afford.
Now, if it weren't for miracles,
I couldn't know my Lord.

"In the morning, O Lord, You will hear my voice."
Psalm 5:3

Be Still

Today I set out on my own
To bring my worship to Your throne,
But stumbled all the way.
I should have left behind my pride
And had Your Spirit at my side,
But I forgot to pray.

Distractions stole away the hours,
Subtle with relentless powers
To keep me from my King.
I had so many things to do
Forgetting that, apart from You
I couldn't do a thing.

With good intentions I would say,
"just let me get this put away,
so I can clear my head."
One thing became another, though,
Until the moon began to show
And it was time for bed.

You could have done the same to me,
But faithfully You set me free.
Your love did not delay.
For You I never wait, but still
You're waiting patiently until
I put my world away.

Although You knew what You'd endure,
Your sacrifice for me was sure.
Your mighty love prevailed.
I'm ever thankful, Lord, to Thee
When You approached the cross for me,
You wouldn't be derailed.

"And the Word became flesh, and dwelt among us, and we saw His glory, glory as of the only begotten from the Father, full of grace and truth." John 1:14

The Once and Forever King

There once was One Who had it all,
Angels at His beck and call.
His praises they would sing.
He sat upon a regal throne.
Righteousness was His alone.
Yes, He had everything.

There once was One who left behind
His riches to pursue the blind-
All those who'd gone astray.
Beginning with a humble birth,
He walked upon this sin-filled earth
To show them all the way.

He talked with sinners face to face
And taught them of His loving grace,
Though He was not esteemed.
He was rejected and opposed,
But followed by a crowd of those
Who hoped to be redeemed.

Knowing that the world was lost,
For every soul He paid the cost
That He alone could pay.
No one could afford the price,
But He, the worthy sacrifice
Took all their sins away.

When His time on earth was done,
He ascended, God's own Son,
To sit at God's right hand.
His Spirit goes with those He sent
And dwells in all who will repent
According to His plan.

"O Lord, my strength and my stronghold, and my refuge in the day of distress." Jeremiah 16:19

Refuge

There stands upon the battle-ground
Throughout this cosmic war
A stronghold for the warriors;
A fortress strong and sure.

Sheltered from relentless storms,
Within its wall of stone,
I find my refuge in the Lord
And will not be alone.

He strengthens my resistance
To the enemy's attack,
While compensating valor
For the certainty I lack.

With mercy always healing,
Providing for my need,
He fills my soul with comfort
And courage to proceed.

When I come to this resting place,
My peace will He restore.
Renewed with strength, well prepared,
I'll face my foe once more.

"For the wages of sin is death." Romans 6:23

Convicted

I stood alone on death row
Convicted of my crime,
Guilty of more than I knew
And almost out of time.

My cellmate there was evil,
Though once he was my friend,
Standing there accusing me
Of what I can't defend.

My jailer led me down the hall
To my electric chair.
How surprised I was to find
That Someone else was there!

He looked into my anguished eyes,
Compassion on His face,
And then assured my pardon
By dying in my place.

Overcome with gratitude
And wonder, I was free.
I want to give myself to Him
As He has done for me.

"But the free gift of God is eternal life in Christ Jesus our Lord." Romans 6:23

The Messenger

My friend, to you I humbly bring
A message from a righteous King,
Its truth is filled with urgency,
Its grace and hope a cause to sing.

As I speak, within I pray
That you will hear the words I say,
That your ears will not be closed
And your heart not turned away.

With your eyes I pray you'll see
The Christ who lives inside of me,
And know He wants for you to live
In Paradise eternally.

You must first confess your sin
And open up your heart to Him.
Believe He died to set you free.
His Spirit will reside within.

This is a gift, you understand,

Offered by His loving hand.
Good works without a saving faith
Are nothing more than grains of sand.

He gave my life a fresh new start.
That's when I vowed to do my part.
I pray that you will now believe
And ask my Lord into your heart.

"Then the Lord commanded the fish." Jonah 2:10

Donna's Dolphins

A true story

As hundreds crowd around the wall
With one united wish,
They hold out their expectant hands
And hope to tempt with fish.

The trainers open up the gates,
The dolphins are released
And now that feeding time is here,
Their hunger has increased.

Yet darting out into the pool,
They hear a higher call
And seek a woman there today
Who has no fish at all.

She sees them not through blinded eyes
But waits uncertainly,

And when she feels it nudge her hand,
Her heart is filled with glee.

It swims around and back again,
Avoiding all the rest,
And rolls its belly up to her,
Allowing her caress.

The others watching are amazed
That in this very hour
A dolphin, right before their eyes,
Has served a higher power.

"Trust in the Lord with all your heart and do not lean on your own understanding." Proverbs 3:3

Faith of a Child

She looks to me with trusting eyes.
Her feelings never need disguise.
Her heart is fresh and dear.
When all her faith on me is hung,
(for she is only six months young)
she has no cause for fear.

One day, she had to get a shot,
And though she may have cried a lot,
She sought me in dismay.
She knew that I would see her through.
When there was nothing else to do,
I'd wipe her tears away.

But through the momentary pain,
Immunity becomes her gain.
Resistance will be strong.
So if a virus should attack,
Her antibodies will fight back,
So how could I go wrong!"

Just like a child we may ask why
The Lord allows our hearts to cry,
But we should only trust.
His reasons, though He may not tell,
Have end results that serve us well.
He knows what's best for us.

"Be on the alert. Your adversary, the devil, prowls around like a roaring lion, seeking someone to devour." 1 Peter 3:8

Warfare

The devil's tactics often hide
Beneath a good disguise.
We need discernment to resist,
To him we must be wise.

For if he came in broad daylight
Announcing it was he
And dressed the part with horns and tail,
Most surely we would flee.

But no, he uses our own mind
And interjects his rage.
Oblivious we think there is
No battle to engage.

He uses situations that
Are everyday but still,
If we react without the Lord,
We choose to do his will.

When, caught up in the snares of life,
We want to shake a fist,
Remember Who has won the war,
And know we can resist!

"Mary has chosen the good part, which shall not be taken away from her." Luke 10:42

Martha and Mary

A woman many years ago
Found her household blessed
When Jesus the Messiah
Had become her welcomed guest.

Excitedly she served Him
Distracted by her deeds
Choosing not His fellowship,
But seeing to His needs.

Her sister sat before the Lord,
His teaching she enjoyed.
The woman who was serving Him
Became a bit annoyed.

"Forgive me, Lord, for saying this,"
she pleaded to her King,
"but shouldn't she be helping me?
She hasn't done a thing."

"Which is your priority?"
He asked her tenderly,
"To fill your time with serving,
or listening to Me?"

"Let your light shine before men in such a way that they may see your good works, and glorify your Father who is in heaven." Matthew 5:16

Lighthouse

The lighthouse warms the summer night
With faithful lights aglow.
A beauty standing on the shore,
She watches to and fro.

A calm inside the raging storm,
She reaches to the sky,
Drawing ships through foggy nights
To harbors safe nearby.

In quiet strength she's standing tall
Above the salty foam.
She sends her light to vessels lost,
Directing them towards home.

An endless beacon through the night,
Her current is divine.
So strengthened is her light within,
She'll never cease to shine.

"To the extent that you did it to one of these brothers of Mine, even the least of them, you did it to Me." Matthew 23:40

Servants of the Lord

My self-reliant spirit learned
Through God's great love outpoured
To set aside my pride and see
The servants of the Lord.

How blessed I was when in my bed,
My strength to be restored,
One by one parading through
Were servants of the Lord.

Through weeks of convalescence
My needs were not ignored,
Not once was I forgotten
By the servants of the Lord.

For all their love and offerings
The Father will reward,
I offer thanks and blessing
To the servants of the Lord.

"She looks well to the ways of her household, and does not eat the bread of idleness." Proverbs 31:27

Proverbs 31

I read through Proverbs 31
And inwardly I grieved.
It seems that such a lofty goal
Could never be achieved.

Sew and plant and stay up late,
It's quite a lot to ask,
But rising up before the sun
Is just an awful task!

These talents I do not possess.
I couldn't sew a stitch
And when it comes to wool and flax-
Don't ask me which is which!

And gardening is not my gift,
As I have often said.
If plants depend on me to grow,
They're bound to wind up dead!

The times are different today,
With different kinds of deeds
For looking after families
And caring for their needs.

The women in our century
Still rise up in the night
When hungry babies cry for them
And children wake with fright.

They cook and clean and rarely rest,
Not even when they're ill.
They teach their children of the Lord
And how to do His will.

The blessings of her family
May seldom reach her ear,
But in their hearts they honor her
And hold this woman dear.

"An excellent wife, who can find?" Proverbs 31:10

No Time for Proverbs 31

A Proverbs 31 poem,
Now what am I to write?
To have the time to read and pray,
I'll rise before daylight.

Alarm goes off, it's five a.m.
No one is awake.
I'll take this quiet time and write,
Should be a piece of cake.

I tap my pencil on my chin
And stare out at the sky.
It's time to take a break, I guess.
I hear a baby cry.

Then after she is fed and changed,
I glance at my notebook.
Can't write my poem right away,
It's time to go and cook.

My husband fed and out the door
And baby back in bed.
The four year old is still asleep,
I now can clear my head.

But thoughts distract me now and then
Of things I need to do.
I lay my notebook on the desk.
I'll just complete a few.

My notebook page throughout the day
Has not yet felt my pen.
I'll wait til they're all back in bed
And try to write it then.

At ten p.m. I fall in bed.
Who needs it anyway?
Of Proverbs 31, I guess
I've nothing wise to say.

"O send out Your light and Your truth, let them lead me,
Let them bring me to Your holy hill and to
Your dwelling places." Psalm 43:3-5

Revival

With scattered thoughts and vacant mind,
I've spent my recent days.
No seeking of His leading hand,
Just floating in a haze.

"Empower me to worship You!"
I cried to Him in tears.
No answer seemed to come to me
From Him who always hears.

I lay my sins before the cross
And begged Him once again,
"Return to me my humble praise,
Don't you remember when?"

Yet silence answered my lament.
I felt so all alone.
"He's left you." nagged my broken heart.
I fell down at His throne.

I picked up His unchanging Word.
He called me through a Psalm.
And through His words He gave
My soul a healing balm.

He drew me back into His light,
Released the tempter's grip,
That through His Spirit I may rest
In God's sweet fellowship.

*"I am forgotten as a dead man, out of mind,
I am like a broken vessel." Psalm 31:12*

Rejected

I thought I understood the world
And people it contained
But then I found Your truth, O God
And what Your love ordained.

The more I got to know You, Lord,
The harder it became
To sympathize with those who thought
They had no cause for blame.

But now I recognize the sins,
Try to walk the other way,
And those who once I called my friends
Tune out the words I say.

It hurts so much sometimes, my Lord,
I don't know what to do.
My loved ones are rejecting me,
Is it because of You?"

Alas, You know the feeling, Lord;
Through tears of pain I see.
The day they crucified You, God,
It was because of me.

*"Even the darkness is not dark to You,
and the night is as bright as the day." Psalm 139:12*

Life Savior

Last night I had a dream of you,
You floated weightless in the sea
Content within its warm embrace
Though powerless, you felt so free

Great dangers lie in wait for you
So many miles away from shore
But, blind to the proximity
You have no fear of what's in store.

Here from my vantage point I see,
Beneath the surface all around,
The deadly terrors stalking you
So close, yet they don't make a sound.

Your help is there, He's reaching out
You see His loving outstretched hand
But you can make it on your own
And by yourself you'll seek dry land.

Because the dangers hide from you,
You're fearless and will not confess
If you refuse His mercy now,
They will consume you nonetheless.

"and lo, I am with You, even to the end of the age."
Matthew 28-20

You Were There

My gracious Lord I was concerned
To tell the things that I had learned
That You revealed to me.
But Precious Savior, You were there,
An answer to an anxious prayer,
Just like I knew You'd be.

I called upon Your promise then,
That You are with me to the end,
And I was not alone.
Because I know Your Word was true,
I put my total trust in You
And now my faith has grown.

I know with certainty that now,
When faced with questions asking how
I know my Savior lives,
That I can confidently say,
"He's right here with me every day,
I know the peace He gives."

When called upon to share Your Word,
I know Your message will be heard,
Your promise I will claim.
My Lord, You know that I am weak,
But You will give me words to speak
To glorify Your name.

"Therefore be on the alert, for you do not know which day your Lord is coming." Matthew 24:42

Prepare the Way

I stumbled, lost in hopeless doubt,
While searching for my own way out
Of sinfulness and shame.
But You refused to let me be,
And saved my soul in spite of me,
Consuming all my blame.

You placed me on Your well-marked trail,
Your Spirit there, to my avail
And sent me on my way
To share Your gift of wondrous grace
And news of that eternal place
That You prepare today.

Amidst the troubles of this land,
You're standing there with outstretched hand
To help me with my task.
Providing me with all my needs
And showing where to plant Your seeds,
I only need to ask.

With loving words and daily prayer,
I witness that You're really there
To all observing me.
And strengthened by Your light within,
I'll show how faithful You have been
And how You've set me free.

I'll not allow my heart to fear,
For You will someday soon appear,
Just as You promised to.
Until that day I'll wait the while,
Praying faithfully that I'll
Prepare the way for You.

"The Lord is not slow about His promise,
but is patient toward you, not wishing for any to perish,
but for all to come to repentance." 2 Peter 3:9

He Has Not Forgotten

You stumble aimlessly through life
Searching for a sign
Of deeper purpose, reason, truth
You cannot seem to find.

You seek fulfillment in your goals
Of pleasure, wealth and fame
And when your efforts fall apart
You seek someone to blame.

Don't you see the path you're on?
How far away you've strayed?
The inner voice He's given you
Will surely start to fade.

Cry out to Him–don't hesitate!
He longs to dry your tears.
His Spirit will sustain you,
Release you from your fears.

He said, "I will return to you."
And though we know not when,
In His perfect time fulfilled,
He'll take us home with Him.

But He has not forgotten you,
His lost and lonely sheep.
He's waiting patiently-repent!
His promise He will keep.

"The god of this world has blinded the minds of the unbelieving so that they might not see the light of the gospel of the glory of Christ, who is the image of God." 2 Corinthians 4:4

Worlds Apart

My dearest friend, I'm sure you know
How close we are, as friendships go.
You're always in my heart.
Though likenesses we gladly toast,
We differ on what matters most-
In faith, we're worlds apart.

While I am resting well-assured
With my eternity secured
In Paradise above,
I worship my eternal King,
Who selflessly did everything
To demonstrate His love.

You rest, unstirred, in worldly views
And, though destruction fills the news,
You find contentment there,
With no one challenging your thoughts,
Imposing with a list of oughts
And rules you find unfair.

It grieves me deeply, friend, to see
How easily you could be free
From fleshly sin and guilt.
Yet constantly you push away
The truth of crucifixion day
On which my faith is built.

I daily bow and pray for you
That, finally, you'll see what's true
And open up your heart.
Accept the Christ Whom I proclaim-
We'll both be living in His Name
No longer worlds apart.

"He chose us in Him before the foundation of the world..." Ephesians 1:4

Blueprint

Before creation of the light,
The heavens, earth and sea,
God had plans in His design
That I would come to be.

Before the earth had sprouted up
With every plant and tree,
He knew my sin would cost His life,
Yet He would set me free.

Before the sun and moon and stars
And even night and day,
He planned for my redemption,
And How He'd make a way.

Before the birds and fish were made,
Before the beasts of land,
Before the serpent came to Eve,
Before the fall of man,

Before the universe we know,
And all the earth we see,
His plans included my own life,
And giving His for me.

"Draw near to God and He will draw near to you." James 4:8

Draw Near

I heard a sad, sad thing today
The news that you have walked away
From 'neath the wings of our sweet Lord
I understand–been there before.

So tired of seeking righteousness,
Of seeing loving friends, no less.
Is this the way it is for you?
I understand–I've felt that, too.

I followed after my desires,
Weakened in the traps of liars
With no one but myself to please,
I fell, with a most frightful ease.

But the ending of the story's good.
You'd love to hear–I know you would.
He saved me from the miry clay
And all I had to do was pray.

A rescue from a fleshly beast.
A miracle, to say the least.
Returning to Him's hard, it's true.
I understand–you know I do.

"For the mountains may be removed and the hills may shake,
but My lovingkindness will not be removed from you."
Isaiah 54:10

Oasis

Does life sometimes seem to beat you down
And when you think you've had enough
And start to stand against attack
To find you're really not so tough?

A brief mirage of empathy
An oasis never meant to stay
A helping hand once offered,
When accepted, quickly fades away

A constant nagging from unlikely source
That what you think you have you don't
And when you think it'll all work out,
You suddenly learn it won't.

A friendly hand you thought was there
To kindly help you rise
Will hold your head down to the floor
And cut you down to size

Do they make you feel less than you are
An unimportant speck
The pleasant life you thought you had
Can seem like such a wreck

Does your contentment fade away
From one insult well-placed?
And make you think you have to prove
Your worth in frenzied haste?

But don't you know who you really are?
Who you became when you believed?
A royal child eternally loved
You'd think you'd be relieved.

How can a world so get you down
When you know you have it all?
Please don't forget when the world attacks
You know just Who to call.

"And the Word became flesh and dwelt among us, and we saw His glory, glory as of the only begotten from the Father, full of grace and truth." John 1:14

One Word

One word it took to bring me down,
One careless, thoughtless one
My self esteem sank through the floor
Emotions came undone

One word they said, that's all it took,
One well-placed hateful word,
Though many other words were said,
That one was all I heard

One word can have such power, it seems,
But they would not have cared
How humble would it make them feel
Had I but these words shared . . .

One word brought sunlight out of dark
And out of oceans, land
One set the universe in place,
One powerful command.

One word made fish and birds and beasts
To live upon this earth
One Word came down to die for me
And show me what I'm worth.

Though other words may bring me down
They will not interfere
God's Word speaks love and peace and truth,
The words I choose to hear.

"For where your treasure is, there your heart will be also."
Matthew 6:21

Rich Little Poor Girl

She walks along, alone again
and feels their judging stare
she shrugs her shoulders, head held high
and really doesn't care

her clothes were handed down to her,
she's never worn them new
her schoolbag was a thrift store find,
her shoes and coat were, too.

Her peers are lavished with the best
From every brand-name store,
And though they mock her hand-me-downs,
She doesn't know she's poor.

Instead she pities those around
Who to their fortunes cling
She feels the best that they can do
is get the next best thing.

Her treasure lies in heaven's gates,
Of this she is assured
Jesus Christ Who also knew
The life that she's endured.

She knows His great redeeming love
That brought Him here to die
and longs to tell them of the best
That money couldn't buy.

*"When you pass through the waters, I will be with you;
and through the rivers, they will not overflow you.
When you walk through the fire, you will not be scorched,
Nor will the flame burn you."* Isaiah 43:2

Through the Fire

I walked along, my head hung low
Alone–or so it seemed
My Lord spoke softly unto me
"My child, you've been redeemed.

Behold, the flaming tongues of fire
You cannot see behind
They crackle, leap and seem to laugh,
They're forceful and unkind.

You feel their heat, at once withdraw
And call to Me in fear
My child, I walk beside you yet,
I've always been right here.

Just take My hand and let Me lead,
I'll take you through the fire
And waiting on the other side,
You'll find your heart's desire."

*"Greater love has no man than this,
that one lay down his life for his friends."* John 15:13

What a Friend

The internet, a magazine
My church, a tv show
All telling me the same old thing
Most everywhere I go
That I should get myself a friend,
As if I didn't know.

A year, two months and several days
Cooped up in this place
No voice to call me on the phone
No helpful friendly face.
I must rely on God alone
And His unending grace.

My door is always open here,
My help I will extend
Had I but one who sought me out,
One solitary friend.
I ask the Lord to draw me close
On Him I must depend.

Perhaps they think I need too much,
Just want a helping hand
And if they offer anything,
Their lives I will demand.
But all I need is just a friend,
A heart to understand.

God's Word reminds my lonely heart,
I have a friend indeed.
Who understands the struggles of
The life I daily lead.
My faithful friend is Jesus Christ,
He'll meet my every need.

"And He has said to me, 'My grace is sufficient for you,.'"
2 Corinthians 12:9

Pondering

At four a.m. the world's asleep
I watch the darkened sky
And ponder my salvation as
The second hand ticks by.

Of Your eternal plans, oh God,
I have so much to learn
I longingly await the day,
Lord, when will You return?

"For all have sinned," Your Word declares
I know that this is true
We work so hard to please ourselves
Instead of pleasing You.

I pray for healing endlessly
As illness takes its toll
So easily forgetful of
The healing of my soul.

"It is better to take refuge in the Lord than to trust in man." Psalm 118:8

Lonely

"I'm forgotten," wrote the Psalmist
his words cut to the bone.
How often do I feel this way
When I'm too long alone?

I sit and wait for others, who
Can give no guarantee
That any given time and place
They'll be right there for me.

"but do not place your trust in man"
Your word so clearly warns,
Yet in my self-indulgent pride
My sulking heart still mourns.

I sadly gaze outside and watch,
Leaves falling to the ground,
Then suddenly I realize
You've always been around.

Just sitting, waiting patiently
For me to come to You.
Could it be that in my silence
You felt forgotten, too?

If I will dwell upon Your truth,
Great peace my soul shall find
That when I feel forgotten, Lord,
It's only in my mind.

Part Two

My Family Beside Me

About the Cover

The flower on the cover of this book is a work of our entire family. The handprints came from Brett and Jodie, then 5 and almost 2. The footprints are Sean and Simon, then only two months old. The leaves in the middle are thumbprints made by Philip and myself. The stem that holds it all together reminds us of Jesus, our vine.

> "I am the vine, you are the branches;
> he who abides in Me, and I in him, he bears much fruit,
> for apart from Me you can do nothing." John 15:5

"I bow my knees before the Father, from Whom every family in heaven and on earth derives its name." Ephesians 3:14-15

Our Family Quilt

One August night in '88
My family began.
Two squares were patched together
When I met my handsome man.

Years passed by and memories
Were sewn into the quilt.
Through struggles and successes,
A strong foundation built.

One joyous day a patch was sewn
In tender shades of blue.
A baby boy was added,
Our family slowly grew.

The quilt begins to take its shape
Like clay before a potter.
Pastels were added on the day
The Lord gave us a daughter.

Then double blessings came to us
Upon my wishful word.
One's name means "God is gracious"
The other means "He heard"

The patchwork of this special quilt
Is precious to behold
Together woven by our Lord
With sturdy threads of gold.

"and He called a child to Himself..." Matthew 18:2

Children

Our children are blessings from heaven above,
Answers to prayer, created with love.
Their presence is welcomed with wide-open arms
As we feed and clothe and protect them from harm.

They may misbehave or speak out of turn,
But by the examples we set they will learn.
So look not upon them as merely décor
Or expect them to quietly sit on the floor.

Encourage their questions and words that they speak
And show them with kindness the answers they seek.
Expect their mistakes as they learn right from wrong
Enjoy all their laughter as you laugh along.

In our home they're priority one
Except for the Lord and our Savior, His Son.
It's here they're accepted and always will be
In the safe loving comfort of their family.

"Train up a child in the way he should go. Even when he is old he will not depart from it." Proverbs 22:6

Little Feet

They wake you with their pitter-patter
And look to you for every need.
Where you've come from does not matter,
These feet will follow where you lead.

"This is the day which the Lord has made,
let us rejoice and be glad in it." Psalm 118:24

Firstborn

Contentedly we stroll along
Humming a familiar song,
His little hand in mine.
Autumn leaves are ever found
Slowly twirling to the ground,
Shades of every kind.

The charming boy, now almost four,
My handsome son whom I adore,
Melts my pondering heart.
I notice not the breezy cold
As I reflect on days of old
When he first got his start.

Into the world he found his way
On a crisp mid-winter day,
A blessing from above.
How could I have ever known
As the threads of life are sewn
That I could be so filled with love?

I think of him in future years,
Imagination threatens tears
As I can see him grown.
The blessings he himself receives
Strolling through the autumn leaves
With a family of his own.

*"Whoever then humbles himself as this child,
he is the greatest in the kingdom of heaven."* Matthew 18:4

Little Missionary

So anxious for the visitor
I knew we'd have today,
I wondered how she would receive
The words I longed to say.

How Jesus' sacrificial gift,
His death upon the cross,
Ensured salvation to the ones
Who made the Lord their boss.

While pondering my nervous thought,
I soon became aware.
My four-year-old was speaking out
The words I had to share!

I heard him say that Jesus died
To save us from our sin
And three days later, he declared,
Our Savior rose again!

My darling child was not concerned
With what she would suppose,
But eagerly began to share,
With joy, all that he knows.

"become like children," Jesus said,
    for child-like faith is true.
   You need only share His love
   And what He's done for you.

"I will give him to the Lord all the days of his life." 1 Samuel 1:11

The Hands Of Time

When newborn, grasped my fingertip
With tiny little fist.
My son then caused my heart to swell,
My eyes to fill with mist.

At ten months, taking his first step
His hands held firm in mine,
Then letting go to step away,
My face did proudly shine.

To wave and clap and blow a kiss,
To whisper secret news.
To throw a ball and catch a fish
And learn to tie his shoes.

Now seated on a yellow bus
And waving out at me,
Those hands, so big now, unafraid
Are all that I can see.

"but if we hope for what we do not see, with perseverance we wait eagerly for it." Romans 8:25

Homecoming

Here sit all his children four
Watching patiently the door
Their hearts are beating to the tune
That daddy will come through it soon.

More precious than a costly gem
Must be the time he spends with them
That they would hasten to his feet,
Forsaking all, this man to greet.

They hear his key, forget their toys,
He's welcomed by his girl and boys
Who rush to him with open arms
Entreating him with all their charms.

Their cheerful race will soon begin,
Though every child will surely win,
Whether be it run or crawl,
For daddy will embrace them all.

"Every perfect gift is from above." James 1:17

Little One

I hold an angel in my arms
While peacefully she sleeps
And with her captivating charms
To my heart she softly speaks.

As I gaze upon her face,
I melt with overwhelming love.
She's yet another gift of grace
From the Father up above.

Her lips will offer up a smile
As if responding to her dreams.
We'll sit and cuddle for a while
The time stands still, or so it seems.

It fills my heart with awe to think,
As I hold my little girl,
There was a mother long ago,
Who held the Savior of the world.

"For power is perfected in weakness." 2 Corinthians 12:9

Surrender

Such trust
When lifted out of cozy bassinet
A fragile babe
Surrendered, with no cause for fret
Held high
Then nestled close to mother's breast
Untouched
By fears and worries will he rest
Secure
Enveloped in her loving arms
His focus
Unaware of lurking harms

Like this small babe, I, too am weak
But calm, when I my Shepherd seek.

"Honor your mother." Exodus 20:12

Mom

I see you in the sands of time
Sprinkled through my life
The pearls of wisdom you have shared
And loving sacrifice.

You're gifted with maternal grace,
Forgiving when I err.
Your gentle kindness and support
Are far beyond compare.

I thank you for the love you show
In everything you do
But even more importantly,
I thank my God for you.

"For the promise is for you and your children and for all those who are far off, as many as the Lord our God will call to Himself." Acts 2:39

Daddy

A father-daughter nature walk
The path is lined with trees
My thoughts go strolling back in time
Through many memories

So many things you did so well
And many things you knew
And when I listened closely, Dad,
I learned a lot from you.

One thing I never understood
Until a recent day
The promise of eternal life–
But you had passed away.

I sought the answers prayerfully
And found one who had shared.
So you had heard the truth of Christ,
But was your heart prepared?

I have to pray for peace of mind,
It's all that I can do.
When Jesus calls me home to Him,
I hope you'll be there, too.

"Bear one another's burdens." Galatians 6:2

Sisters in Christ

We're kindred spirits, you and I
We talk of everything
We'll lean upon each other through
The troubles life can bring.

We both have seen this wretched world
In ways we might regret
A common thread that draws us near,
We're willing to forget.

As we've relied upon the Lord
And made His ways our own,
He provides a place for us
To kneel before His throne.

The prayer requests that we will share
Throughout our sisterhood
Are heard by Him who answers them
For our eternal good.

We're drawn together by His plan,
I hope you will agree
A blessing out of heaven's grace
As friends eternally.

"Let us not lose heart in doing good, for in due time we will reap if we do not grow weary." Galatians 6:9

A World of Influence

We dream of growing up someday
And having brilliant things to say
And great influence widely sewn
To change the world from what we've known.

In school we study physics laws
And orate to a vast applause
And dream of what we'll someday be
And how we'll change the world we see.

God may have plans amidst it all
To make our borders very small;
The world of influence He intends
Is wrapped up in the gifts He sends.

There, everything we do is heard,
Our every action, every word.
We'll shape a future brilliant mind
To change the world by God's design.

"As God has distributed to each one, as the Lord has called each one, so let him walk." 1 Corinthians 7:17

Resume

Alumni updates come to me
From my university.
Ambitious grads have ventured out
In search of worldly wealth and clout.

Doctors, lawyers, scientists,
Authors on the top ten lists.
They send to me a questionnaire
On what I've done since I went there.

My first reaction comes in haste,
Was my tuition all a waste?
What will all those people say?
I stay home with my kids all day!

So, lest they think I'm just a slob,
I thought about my chosen job
And then wrote out a resume
Describing what I do all day.

Accountant, chef, nutritionist,
To name a few on my long list,
Consultant, nurse, interpreter,
Top advisor and chauffer.

I span the range of big and small
And, without limit, do it all.
No need to specialize in one,
Variety is much more fun.

My hours never end, it seems.
Up at night, no time for dreams
No timecard to punch in or out
And lunch breaks I must do without.

But hugs and giggles serve as pay
And watching children run and play.
I see them grow and learn and smile-
And that's what makes it all worthwhile.

"All the ways of a man are clean in his own sight, but the Lord weighs the motives." Proverbs 16:2

Life Happens Here

Welcome friends, please come inside,
We're glad you came today
Watch your step as you walk through,
Some toys are in your way.

You will not find this place of ours
Sterile and dust-free,
And you'll find dishes in the sink
I almost guarantee.

A pile of laundry (Dirty? Clean?)
You almost always find.
I'm sure you'll see much evidence,
My housework falls behind.

If this is what you're here to see,
Go ahead, inspect
Beyond the mess there's order, though,
That you might not expect.

See the children playing here?
They're happy and secure
Though outwardly they're smudged a bit,
Inside their hearts, they're pure.

Observe how much they like to read
Just hear them laugh and sing,
admire their artwork on the walls
and feel the hugs they bring.

You are welcome to decide,
To see each flaw and smear
Or look beyond where beauty lies,
In the life that happens here.

"I am my beloved's, and his desire is for me."
Song of Solomon 7:10

The Dance

She gazed at him with loving eyes,
His like sparkling fireflies.
She's beautiful, he's debonair.
They re-ignite their love affair.

A teasing smile, a knowing wink
Onlookers don't know what to think.
They're tuning out the world around
And basking in the love they've found.

He takes her hand and leads her in
She can't believe how long it's been.
As the band begins to play
Dancers meet and start to sway.

He glides her gently 'cross the floor.
All others there they both ignore.
Much time has passed, a decade now
They re-affirm their sacred vow.

Many have to reminisce
To reclaim feelings that they miss
But these need not remember when
Each day they fall in love again.

Part Three

The World Around Me

My Stand

The poetry in this section is mostly about political or social themes. Each was inspired by specific events or comments people have made which, I feel, show the way the world views these themes in contrast to God's view.

A Perfect World, for example, was written in response to a comment I heard, where a woman said in a perfect world, divorced parents would live in the same town so their children could see both equally. Have we lowered our standards? There was a time when a perfect world would have been one without any divorce at all!

Madeline's Legacy is about Madeline O'Hare, who had prayer taken out of school. A Closer Look is a response to some disturbing anti-Christian song lyrics I saw somewhere. To Speak is my answer to a friend who thought it was arrogant for someone to say they *know* they are going to heaven. This is not an arrogant claim, but a truly humble one, because it means you have trusted that Christ has done everything that needs to be done and there is nothing you can do to earn your salvation. It is a gift, bought and paid for by the Giver. How can it be arrogant to accept a gift?

Overall, truth is truth. You don't have to believe it to make it true. There is such comfort in that! Praise God for His faithfulness!

Finally, Longing is my anticipation of what is to come. The Lord Jesus will return and I can't wait!

"And do not be conformed to this world, but be transformed by the renewing of your mind, so that you may prove what the will of God is, that which is good and acceptable and perfect."
Romans 12:2

Will I Have to Stand?

The evening news invades my home,
I reach for my remote.
I try to pacify myself
A lump forms in my throat.

Ignore the vast chaotic world
And close myself inside.
Secure in my own destiny,
But still compelled to hide.

It's coming to an end, they say,
The Lord will soon return
Watch for Him, the Bible says,
His Kingdom's our concern.

I tremble in my cowardice
And watch the world outside.
Christians standing for the truth,
I'm still compelled to hide.

It's easier to block it out
And make up some excuse
For knowing nothing of the world
And Satan's cruel abuse.

I wonder if the time will come
When I will have to stand,
I need to claim His promises,
Pull my head out of the sand.

Get out! Go! Stop wasting time!
This is no time to hide!
Take up my cross and follow Him,
And in His peace abide.

*"I am the way, the truth and the life;
no one comes to the Father but through Me." John 14:6*

Truth Is Truth

The truth is what you make of it,
So many people say.
Create your own reality
As your beliefs convey.

This attitude for life has been
Adopted far and wide.
To be politically correct,
The truth must be denied.

With so much ambiguity,
Our politicians stand
For nothing in particular,
To get their votes in hand.

Amidst this moral drought we need
A rebel with a cause,
A man who'll stand for Jesus Christ,
And do so without pause.

A president who's not afraid
To speak the gospel truth
Could bring our country back to God
And redirect its youth.

Truth is truth, you can't escape it,
Though it may seem mundane.
However unacceptable,
The truth will still remain

*"What therefore God has joined together,
Let no man separate."* Matthew 19:6

A Perfect World

"In a perfect world," she said-
It made me want to cry
"children of divorce can live
with absent dad nearby."

A 'perfect world'–imagine that!
What have we come to now?
When 'perfect world' is not defined
By holding to a vow!

What do we teach them by our deeds-
These children we adore-
"the one whom I loved yesterday,
Today I love no more"?

That people they most trust are weak,
And sometimes they may roam?
No! To a child "perfect world"
Is mom and dad at home!

"Resist the devil and he will flee from you." James 4:7

Madeline's Legacy

Beware! An influential one
Has issues yet to vent.
How can it be that one so lost
Controls our government?

One nation, under God, we say
With hands upon our hearts.
We're indivisible, yet one
Can tear our world apart.

She takes her stand, an atheist,
And with the words she'll say,
She'll tear down our foundations
While she takes our rights away.

"In God we trust", will that be next?
It makes me sick to think.
Remove it from our currency
Why not? We're on the brink.

Our founding fathers worked so hard
To make our country free.
Yet, still it all comes down to this;
Resist and she will flee!

"For You formed my inward parts. You wove me in my mother's womb." Psalm 139:13

Heaven's Child

Our children are blessings from heaven above
Gifts from the Father, created with love.
Ours to be welcomed with wide-open arms-
Dependent on us to protect them from harm.

His from conception, a beautiful soul
To play an eternally valuable role
Predestined before He created the earth-
Amazing that one life contains so much worth!

We safeguard their future in every respect,
Incarcerate those who abuse and neglect,
Protect the environment so they'll have trees,
And immunize them against every disease.

Yet our culture condones the most cruel abuse
With vanity, choice, and most any excuse.
They look at His treasures, "no, thank you." They say,
Then seek out a doctor to take it away.

When babies cannot look to parents with trust
And government fails them, then it's up to us.
We need to speak out with one resonant voice,
That God-given life's not a matter of choice!

"Even though I walk through the valley of the shadow of death, I will fear no evil, for You are with me." Psalm 23:4

September 11, 2001

A nation mourns a tragic loss
My heart is truly grieved
I give my sadness to the Lord
In whom I have believed.

Though anger pulses through my veins,
Revenge in every thought,
I give my anger to Him too
His justice fails me not.

With talk of terrorist attacks,
My mind is plagued with fright,
But rest I must beneath His wings,
For He holds far more might.

Uncertainly envelopes us
What does our future hold?
He's promised that, if we believe,
We'll walk on streets of gold.

"You shall have no other gods before Me." Exodus 20:3

Who Is This God?

Who is this god that you pray to,
When your world seems so unsure?
Does he set your feet upon solid ground
And make your life secure?

Was he created by your hands
And vain imagination?
Or did he create you,
Your world, your very nation?

Will your god hear you
Wherever you may go?
At any moment, day or night,
Or do you even know?

Does your god let you be
Without a word to speak,
While you do whatever you please?
Tell me, is he that weak?

Will he let you tear your world apart,
By tolerating sin,
Or is he a god of justice
Who will never let evil win?

Does your god give life
And truth and inner peace?
Does he come from eternity
Where his days will never cease?

Who is this god that you pray to?
Does he have an eternal throne?
Is he able to forgive at great expense,
Being crucified by is own?

Can your god give you the promise
Of everlasting life,
By simply believing in his name
And painful sacrifice?

If your god doesn't give you assurance
And he's come from your own design
And he hasn't the power to sustain you,
Then please let me tell you about mine!

"at the name of Jesus, every knee will bow." Philippians 2:10

Everybody Bows

The godless world so many seek
Is never to be found.
They may deny the one true God,
Yet other gods abound.

They might not worship gods by name.
They've made no solemn vow,
But something means the world to them,
And to that god they bow.

For freedom they might risk their lives.
For work they sacrifice.
For money they will sell their souls
Regardless of the price.

An atheist does not exist
(to this they raise their brows).
Though it may be to worldly things,
Yes, everybody bows!

The time will come when they'll forget
The gods they worship now
And to the one true living God,
Every knee shall bow.

*"And this I pray, that your love may abound still more
and more in real knowledge and all discernment."*
Philippians 1:9

Line It Up

A preacher stands upon the stage
The crowds have come to hear
Eloquent and worldly wise
Yet spiritually unclear.

He quotes a teacher he adores
His Bible's set aside.
They hang upon his every word
Their minds are open wide.

The words he speaks make perfect sense
How could they doubt it's true?
Without dispute, they'll never know
He's teaching something new.

Put the spirits to the test
God's holy Word is clear.
Line it up against His Truth.
Test every word you hear.

God's told us all we need to know,
His words can be believed
Use discernment, seek the truth,
And you won't be deceived.

"Blessed is the nation whose God is the Lord." Psalm 33:12

The Fourth of July

Today's the monumental date,
our freedom we will celebrate.
We'll honor those whose blood was cast
to give us liberty at last.

They bravely went onto the field,
perhaps they knew their fate was sealed,
yet, still they vowed to make us free,
then fought and died unselfishly.

Today you can remember, too,
that Someone else has died for you,
to set you free from sin and shame,
He took upon Himself your blame.

Our precious Savior Jesus Christ,
the only worthy sacrifice,
came down from heaven just for us,
and all we have to do is trust!

With gratitude to Him Most High,
enjoy freedom this July,
and it will be for you, I pray,
a blessed Independence Day!

"But sanctify Christ as Lord in your hearts, always being ready to make a defense to everyone who asks you to give an account for the hope that is in you, yet with gentleness and reverence." 1 Peter 3:15

A Closer Look

Someone told you it was wrong
Somewhere, hidden in a song,
You found your comfort in his cries
And instantly believed his lies.

Who wrote that song you hold on to?
What will that singer do for you?
His anti-Jesus, angry claim
Is a religion just the same.

His bitter words say I'm a slave
Just listen to him rant and rave!
Slave, he calls me, to a Book.
I challenge you to take a look.

The Book that he is singing of
Is not of bondage, but of love.
The reason Christ was crucified,
The reason that he bled and died,

His only purpose on this earth
To show you how much you are worth!
He didn't buy us slavery
But paid that price to set us free!

"These things I have written to you who believe in the name of the Son of God, so that you may know that you have eternal life." 1 John 5:13

To Speak

"It's arrogant," they say
"all the answers on his tongue."
"Stop teaching us," they taunt him so,
"the school bell hasn't rung!"

Misunderstood, he bows his head
To seek direction wise
When should he speak and when be still
And when expose the lies?

Too soon and they may run away,
"He's preaching yet again!"
too late, he fears they'll miss their chance,
despair would surely win.

"Not grace!" they cry, "how could it be?"
"There's something I must do."
Insisting they can earn God's love,
"The one who's lost is you!"

Arrogant was what they said
Of truths he had to tell.
To think it's something you can earn
Is arrogance as well.

"The grass withers, the flower fades, but the word of our God stands forever." Isaiah 40:8

Debate

It stood up straight, its branches full
And strong in gentle breeze;
A monument stretched to the sky
No furied storm could seize.

The winds attack in futile hope
To drive it from its root;
Stirring up chaotic doubt
That few would dare refute.

Its roots not merely holding fast,
But deepening despite.
The tree stands stronger in the wake
When clouds give way to light.

"And they will see the Son of Man coming on the clouds of the sky with power and great glory." Matthew 24:30

Longing

This morning dawned a dreary grey,
Yet couldn't steal my joy away,
As You were on my mind.
My thought of You uplifted me
To higher heights than I could see
And treasures yet to find.

Dreams of never-ending light
Had given me, throughout the night
A yearning in my soul
For the day I'll see Your face,
In heaven You've prepared a place
Where You will make me whole.

I long to see You in the sky
Coming to receive me, I
Anticipate the day.
Eternally I'll be with You,
Beautiful my Savior who
Took all my sin away.

Just knowing of the streets of gold
And heaven's beauty to behold
Just fills my heart with glee.
Whatever treasures life bestows
Can't possibly compare to those
You have in store for me.

Made in the USA
Middletown, DE
26 November 2021